FLOWERS

ORCHIDS

John F. Prevost
ABDO & Daughters

Published by Abdo & Daughters, 4940 Viking Drive, Suite 622, Edina, Minnesota 55435.

Copyright © 1996 by Abdo Consulting Group, Inc., Pentagon Tower, P.O. Box 36036, Minneapolis, Minnesota 55435 USA. International copyrights reserved in all countries. No part of this book may be reproduced in any form without written permission from the publisher.

Printed in the United States.

Cover Photo credits: Peter Arnold, Inc.
Interior Photo credits: Peter Arnold, Inc.

Edited by Bob Italia

Library of Congress Cataloging-in-Publication Data

Prevost, John F.
    Orchids / John F. Prevost.
    p. cm. -- (Flowers)
    Includes index.
    Summary: Describes the habitat, parts, pests and diseases, and varieties of orchids.
    ISBN 1-56239-609-9
    1. Orchids--Juvenile literature. [1. Orchids.] I. Title. II. Series: Prevost, John F.
    Flowers
    QK495.064P75 1996
    584' .15--dc20
                                   96-3800
                                         CIP
                                         AC

Contents

Orchids and Family

Orchids are among the largest plant **families** in the world. They grow worldwide wherever there is water. Most wild orchids like **tropical climates**. A few types grow north of the Arctic Circle, in Canada, and Alaska.

Many orchid types are **threatened** or **endangered**. These plants should not be picked or collected. If their **habitats** are disturbed, they will die.

Many people grow tropical orchids in homes or **greenhouses**. Some orchids can grow outdoors if the climate and soil are right.

Opposite page:
Orchid flowers have
unusual shapes.

Roots, Soil, and Water

Orchid plants have different root types. Some **tropical** orchids grow on tree bark or branches to get closer to sunlight. These are called air plants. Their roots grow above the ground, not in the soil. They get **minerals** and **nutrients** from rainwater. They do not hurt the trees on which they grow.

Most warm-weather orchids grow in the ground. Roots hold the plants upright. There are many different root types. Some are thick and tube-shaped. Others are long and thin and grow in special soil. Planting them in different soil causes **root rot**, and the plants will die.

Orchids grow in many types of soil.

Stems, Leaves, and Sunlight

Sunlight is important to every green plant. Plants use sunlight to change water, **nutrients,** and air into food and **oxygen**. This process is called **photosynthesis**.

The stems support the leaves and flowers. Ground water travels from the roots through the stems and into the leaves. The leaves make food that travels through the stems and into the roots. Many orchids also use their roots or stems to store food and water.

Not all orchids have leaves or stems. Some have green roots, where photosynthesis takes place. A few orchids do not need sunlight. They get their food from **decaying** matter.

Photosynthesis

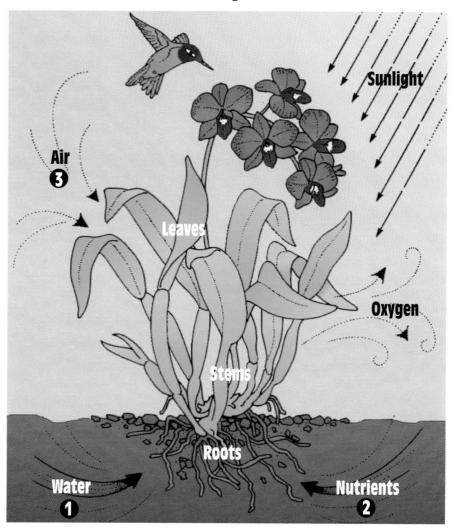

Ground water (1) and nutrients (2) travel through the roots and stems and into the leaves where air (3) is drawn in. Then the plant uses sunlight to change these three elements into food and oxygen.

Flowers

Many people grow orchids because of the flowers, which have all kinds of colors, scents, shapes, and sizes. A simple type is the Lady's-slipper. More than 12 flowers may grow on each stem.

The orchid flower has three main parts: the **petal**, the **stamen,** and the **pistil**. The petals help protect the flower. The stamen makes **pollen** used to **fertilize** the pistil's **ovules,** which grow into seeds.

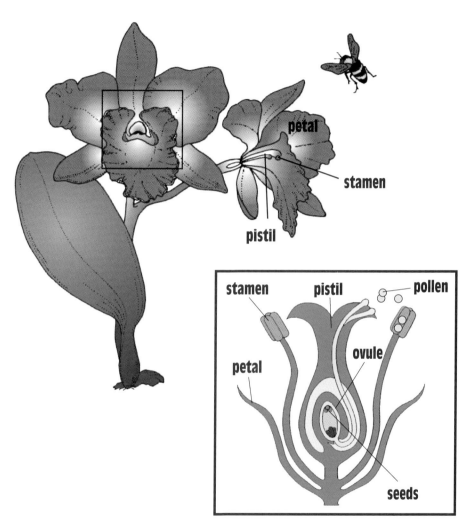

The stamen makes pollen that fertilizes the pistil's ovules.
The fertilized ovules then grow into seeds.

Seeds

The three chambers of the flower's **ovary** contain the seeds. As they ripen, the chambers swell into **capsules,** which split and release thousands of tiny seeds. Inside each seed is an **embryo** from which the plant is born. The seed must land in the right spot on the ground for the plant to grow and survive.

Because orchid seeds are among the smallest in the plant world, winds can carry them high into the air. Some orchid seeds have been found on weather balloons!

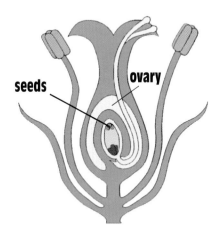

seeds

ovary

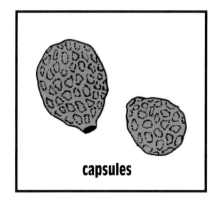

capsules

seeds

The orchid's ovary swells into capsules. Each capsule contains thousands of tiny seeds.

Insects and Other Friends

Some insects are good for plants. The orchid's flower color and smell will attract these helpful insects. Many flowers have lips on which the insects land. Some flowers make **nectar** to reward the insect with a small meal.

When the insect leaves, it is covered with **pollen**. When the pollen-covered insect lands on another plant's flower, it **fertilizes** the plant.

Flowers also attract other animals. Hummingbirds and small mice help **pollinate** orchids as they travel from flower to flower in search of food. Without help from these creatures, orchids could not **reproduce**.

The bright colors of the orchids attract insects.

Pests and Diseases

Some insects are harmful to orchid plants. They chew orchids and suck the juice out of leaves, roots, and stems. If not controlled, insect pests will kill the plant.

There are many safe ways to keep pests away. **Poisons** and **predatory** insects work well.

Diseases may attack weak or damaged plants. Sometimes insects will spread diseases as they eat plants.

Many different insects eat orchids.

Varieties

There are more than 240 types of orchids in the world. More are discovered each year. Over the past 200 years, people have grown new **varieties**.

Some orchids do not make seeds. They are grown from their own **tissue**.

Opposite page:
Orchid varieties are among
the favorites of flower
lovers around the world.

19

Orchids and
the Plant Kingdom

The plant kingdom is divided into several groups, including flowering plants, fungi, plants with bare seeds, and ferns.

 Flowering plants grow flowers to make seeds. These seeds often grow inside protective ovaries or fruit.

 Fungi are plants without leaves, flowers, or green coloring, and cannot make their own food. They include mushrooms, molds, and yeast.

 Plants with bare seeds (such as evergreens and conifers) do not grow flowers. Their seeds grow unprotected, often on the scale of a cone.

 Ferns are plants with roots, stems, and leaves. They do not grow flowers or seeds.

There are two groups of flowering plants: monocots (MAH-no-cots) and dicots (DIE-cots). Monocots have seedlings with one leaf. Dicots have seedlings with two leaves.

The orchid family is one type of monocot. All orchid varieties are part of the orchid family.

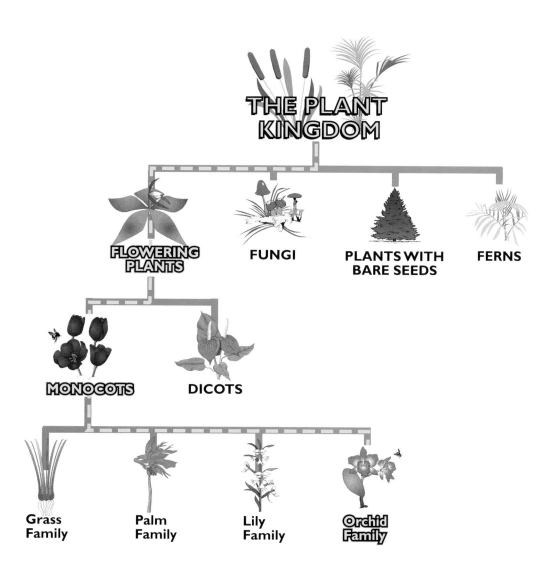

THE PLANT KINGDOM

FLOWERING PLANTS

FUNGI

PLANTS WITH BARE SEEDS

FERNS

MONOCOTS

DICOTS

Grass Family

Palm Family

Lily Family

Orchid Family

21

Glossary

capsule (CAP-sool) - The tiny plant part that holds seeds.

climate - The kind of weather a place has.

decay (de-KAY) - To become rotten.

disease (diz-EEZ) - A sickness.

embryo (EM-bree-oh) - A plant in the early stage of development, before sprouting from a seed.

endangered - Near extinction.

family - A group of related living things.

fertilize (FUR-tuh-lize) - The process of making the ovule able to develop into a seed.

greenhouse - A building made for growing plants.

habitat - A place where a living thing is found naturally.

minerals - Substances that are not plants, animals, or other living things.

nectar (NECK-tar) - A sweet fluid found in some flowers.

nutrients (NEW-tree-ents) - Substances that help a plant grow and keep it healthy.

ovary (OH-va-ree) - The part of a flower where seeds grow.

ovules (AH-vules) - Seeds before they are fertilized by pollen.

oxygen (OX-ih-jen) - A gas without color, taste, or odor found in air and water.

petal - One of several leaves that protect the flower's center.

photosynthesis (foe-toe-SIN-thuh-sis) - The use of sunlight to make food.

pistil - The female (seed-making) flower part.

poison (POY-zun) - A substance that is dangerous to life or health.

pollen - A yellow powder that fertilizes flowers.

pollinate (PAHL-ih-nate) - The use of pollen to fertilize a flower.

predator (PRED-uh-tore) - An animal that eats other animals.

reproduce (re-pro-DUCE) - To produce offspring.

root rot - A decay that attacks the roots.

stamen (STAY-men) - The male flower part (the flower part that makes pollen).

threatened - Almost endangered.

tissue - The substance that forms the parts of living things.

tropical (TRAH-pih-kull) - The hottest climate on earth.

varieties (vuh-RIE-uh-teez) - Different types of plants that are closely related.

Index